I0004965

Book 1
Python Programming
Professional Made Easy

BY SAM KEY

&

Book 2
HTML Professional
Programming Made Easy

BY SAM KEY

Book 1
Python Programming
Professional Made Easy

By Sam Key

Expert Python Programming Language Success in a Day for Any Computer User!

Programming Box Set #50: Python Programming Professional Made Easy & HTML Professional Programming Made Easy

Copyright 2015 by Sam Key - All rights reserved.

In no way is it legal to reproduce, duplicate, or transmit any part of this document in either electronic means or in printed format. Recording of this publication is strictly prohibited and any storage of this document is not allowed unless with written permission from the publisher. All rights reserved.

Table Of Contents

Introduction

I want to thank you and congratulate you for purchasing the book, "Python Programming Professional Made Easy: Expert Python Programming Language Success in a Day for Any Computer User!"

This book contains proven steps and strategies on how to program Python in a few days. The lessons ingrained here will serve as an introduction to the Python language and programming to you. With the little things you will learn here, you will still be able to create big programs.

The book is also designed to prepare you for advanced Python lessons. Make sure that you take note of all the pointers included here since they will help you a lot in the future.

Thanks again for purchasing this book. I hope you enjoy it!

Chapter 1: Introduction to Programming Languages

This short section is dedicated to complete beginners in programming. Knowing all the things included in this chapter will lessen the confusion that you might encounter while learning Python or any programming language.

Computers do not know or cannot do anything by itself. They just appear smart because of the programs installed on them.

Computer, Binary, or Machine Language

You cannot just tell a computer to do something using human language since they can only understand computer language, which is also called machine or binary language. This language only consists of 0's and 1's.

On the other hand, you may not know how to speak or write computer language. Even if you do, it will take you hours before you can tell a computer to do one thing since just one command may consist of hundreds or thousands of 1's and 0's. If you translate one letter in the human alphabet to them, you will get two or three 1's or 0's in return. Just imagine how many 1's and 0's you will need to memorize if you translate a sentence to computer language.

Assembly or Low Level Programming Language

In order to overcome that language barrier, programmers have developed assemblers. Assemblers act as translators between a human and a computer.

However, assemblers cannot comprehend human language. They can only translate binary language to assembly language and vice versa. So, in order to make use of assemblers, programmers need to learn their language, which is also called a low level language.

Unfortunately, assembly language is difficult to learn and memorize. Assembly language consists of words made from mnemonics that only computer experts know. And for one to just make the computer display something to the screen, a programmer needs to type a lot of those words.

High Level Programming Language

Another solution was developed, and that was high level programming languages such as C++, Java, and Python. High level programming languages act as a translator for humans and assembly language or humans to computer language.

Unlike assembly language (or low level language), high level programming languages are easier to understand since they commonly use English words instead of mnemonics. With it, you can also write shorter lines of codes since they already provide commonly used functions that are shortened into one or two keywords.

If you take one command or method in Python and translate it to assembly language, you will have long lines of codes. If you translate it to computer language, you will have thousands of lines composed of 1's and 0's.

In a nutshell, high level programming languages like Python are just translators for humans and computers to understand each other. In order for computers to do something for humans, they need to talk or instruct them via programming languages.

Many high level languages are available today. Among the rest, Python is one of the easiest languages to learn. In the next chapter, you will learn how to speak and write with Python language for your computer to do your bidding.

Chapter 2: Getting Prepped Up

On the previous chapter, you have learned the purpose of programming languages. By choosing this book, you have already decided that Python is the language that you want to use to make your programs. In this chapter, your learning of speaking, writing, and using this language starts.

You, Python, and Your Computer

Before you start writing, take a moment to understand the relationship between you, the programming language, and the computer. Imagine that you are a restaurant manager, and you have hired two foreign guys to cook for the restaurant, which is the program you want to create. The diners in your restaurant are the users of your program.

The first guy is the chef who only knows one language that you do not know. He follows recipes to the letter, and he does not care if the recipe includes him jumping off the cliff. That guy is your computer.

The second guy is the chef's personal translator who will translate the language you speak or write, which is Python, to the language the chef knows. This translator is strict and does not tolerate typos in the recipes he translates. If he finds any mistake, he will tell it right to your face, walk away with the chef, and leave things undone.

He also does not care if the recipe tells the chef to run on circles until he dies. That is how they work. This guy is your programming language.

Since it is a hassle to tell them the recipe while they cook, you decided to write a recipe book instead. That will be your program's code that the translator will read to the chef.

Installing Python

You got two things to get to program in Python. First, get the latest release of Python. Go to this website: https://www.python.org/downloads/.

Download Python 3.4.2 or anything newer than that. Install it. Take note of the directory where you will install Python.

Once you are done with the installation, you must get a source code editor. It is recommended that you get Notepad++. If you already have a source code editor, no need to install Notepad++, too. To download Notepad++, go to: http://www.notepad-plus-plus.org/download/v6.6.9.html. Download and install it.

Version 2.x or 3.x

If you have already visited the Python website to download the program, you might have seen that there are two Python versions that you can download. As of this writing, the first version is Python 3.4.2 and the second version is Python 2.7.8.

About that, it is best that you get the latest version, which is version 3.4.2. The latest version or build will be the only one getting updates and fixes. The 2.7.8 was already declared as the final release for the 2.x build.

Beginners should not worry about it. It is recommended that new Python programmers start with 3.x or later before thinking about exploring the older versions of Python.

Programming and Interactive Mode

Python has two modes. The first one is Programming and the second one is Interactive. You will be using the Interactive mode for the first few chapters of this book. On the other hand, you will be using the Programming mode on the last few chapters.

In Interactive mode, you can play around with Python. You can enter lines of codes on it, and once you press enter, Python will immediately provide a feedback or execute the code you input. To access Python's interactive mode, go to the directory where you installed Python and open the Python application. If you are running on Windows, just open the Run prompt, enter python, and click OK.

In Programming mode, you can test blocks of code in one go. Use a source editor to write the program. Save it as a .py file, and run it as Python program. In Windows, .py files will be automatically associated with Python after you install Python. Due to that, you can just double click the file, and it will run.

Chapter 3: Statements

A program's code is like a recipe book. A book contains chapters, paragraphs, and sentences. On the other hand, a program's code contains modules, functions, and statements. Modules are like chapters that contain the recipes for a full course meal. Procedures or functions are like paragraphs or sections that contain recipes. Statements are like the sentences or steps in a recipe. To code a program with Python, you must learn how to write statements.

Statements

Statements are the building blocks of your program. Each statement in Python contains one instruction that your computer will follow. In comparison to a sentence, statements are like imperative sentences, which are sentences that are used to issue commands or requests. Unlike sentences, Python, or programming languages in general, has a different syntax or structure.

For example, type the statement below on the interpreter:

print("Test")

Press the enter key. The interpreter will move the cursor to the next line and print 'Test' without the single quotes. The command in the sample statement is print. The next part is the details about the command the computer must do. In the example, it is ("test"). If you convert that to English, it is like you are commanding the computer to print the word Test on the program.

Python has many commands and each of them has unique purpose, syntax, and forms. For example, type this and press enter:

1 + 1

Python will return an answer, which is 2. The command there is the operator plus sign. The interpreter understood that you wanted to add the two values and told the computer to send the result of the operation.

Variables

As with any recipe, ingredients should be always present. In programming, there will be times that you would want to save some data in case you want to use them later in your program. And there is when variables come in.

Variables are data containers. They are the containers for your ingredients. You can place almost any type of data on them like numbers or text. You can change the value contained by a variable anytime. And you can use them anytime as long as you need them.

To create one, all you need is to think of a name or identifier for the variable and assign or place a value to it. To create and assign a value to variables, follow the example below:

example1 = 10

On the left is the variable name. On the right is the value you want to assign to the variable. If you just want to create a variable, you can just assign 0 to the variable to act as a placeholder. In the middle is the assignment operator, which is the equal sign. That operator tells the interpreter that you want him to assign a value, which is on its right, to the name or object on the left.

To check if the variable example1 was created and it stored the value 10 in it, type the variable name on the interpreter and press enter. If you done it correctly, the interpreter will reply with the value of the variable. If not, it will reply with a NameError: name <variable_name> is not defined. It means that no variable with that name was created.

Take note, you cannot just create any name for a variable. You need to follow certain rules to avoid receiving syntax errors when creating them. And they are:

> Variable names should start with an underscore or a letter.
> Variable names must only contain letters, numbers, or underscores.
> Variable names can be one letter long or any length.
> Variable names must not be the same with any commands or reserved keywords in Python.
> Variable names are case sensitive. The variable named example1 is different from the variable named Example1.

As a tip, always use meaningful names for your variables. It will help you remember them easily when you are writing long lines of codes. Also, keep them short and use only one style of naming convention. For example, if you create a variable like thisIsAString make sure that you name your second variable like that too: thisIsTheSecondVariable not this_is_the_second_variable.

You can do a lot of things with variables. You can even assign expressions to them. By the way, expressions are combinations of numbers and/or variables together with operators that can be evaluated by the computer. For example:

Example1 = 10

Example2 = 5 + 19

Example3 = Example1 - Example2

If you check the value of those variables in the interpreter, you will get 10 for Example1, 24 for Example2, and -14 for Example3.

Chapter 4: Basic Operators – Part 1

As of this moment, you have already seen three operators: assignment (=), addition (+), and subtraction (-) operators. You can use operators to process and manipulate the data and variables you have – just like how chefs cut, dice, and mix their ingredients.

Types of Python Operators

Multiple types of operators exist in Python. They are:

- ➤ **Arithmetic**
- ➤ **Assignment**
- ➤ **Comparison**
- ➤ **Logical**
- ➤ **Membership**
- ➤ **Identity**
- ➤ **Bitwise**

Up to this point, you have witnessed how arithmetic and assignment operators work. During your first few weeks of programming in Python, you will be also using comparison and logical operators aside from arithmetic and assignment operators. You will mostly use membership, identity, and bitwise later when you already advanced your Python programming skills.

As a reference, below is a list of operators under arithmetic and assignment. In the next chapter, comparison and logical will be listed and discussed briefly in preparation for later lessons.

For the examples that the list will use, x will have a value of 13 and y will have a value of 7.

Arithmetic

Arithmetic operators perform mathematical operations on numbers and variables that have numbers stored on them.

> **+ : Addition. Adds the values besides the operator.**

  z = 13 + 7

  z's value is equal to 20.

> **- : Subtraction. Subtracts the values besides the operator.**

  z = x – y

  z's value is equal to 6.

* : Multiplication. Multiplies the values besides the operator.

$z = x * y$

z's value is equal to 91.

/ : Division. Divides the values besides the operator.

$z = x / y$

z's value is equal to 1.8571428571428572.

** : Exponent. Applies exponential power to the value to the left (base) with the value to the right (exponent).

$z = x ** y$

z's value is equal to 62748517.

// : Floor Division. Divides the values besides the operator and returns a quotient with removed digits after the decimal point.

$z = x // y$

z's value is equal to 1.

% : Modulus. Divides the values besides the operator and returns the remainder instead of the quotient.

$z = x \% y$

z's value is equal to 6.

Assignment

Aside from the equal sign or simple assignment operator, other assignment operators exist. Mostly, they are combinations of arithmetic operators and the simple assignment operator.

They are used as shorthand methods when reassigning a value to a variable that is also included in the expression that will be assigned to it. Using them in your code simplifies and makes your statements clean.

= : Simple assignment operator. It assigns the value of the expression on its right hand side to the variable to its left hand side.

$z = x + y * x - y \% x$

z's value is equal to 97.

The following assignment operators work like this: it applies the operation first on the value of the variable on its left and the result of the expression on its right. After that, it assigns the result of the operation to the variable on its left.

+= : Add and Assign

x += y

x's value is equal to 20. It is equivalent to x = x + y.

-= : Subtract and Assign

x -= y

x's value is equal to 6. It is equivalent to x = x − y.

*= : Multiply and assign

x *= y

x's value is equal to 91. It is equivalent to x = x * y.

/= : Divide and assign

x /= y

x's value is equal to 1.8571428571428572. It is equivalent to x = x / y.

**= : Exponent and Assign

x **= y

x's value is equal to 62748517. It is equivalent to x = x ** y.

//= : Floor Division and Assign

x //= y

x's value is equal to 1. It is equivalent to x = x // y.

%= : Modulus and Assign

x %= y

x's value is equal to 6. It is equivalent to x = x % y.

Multiple Usage of Some Operators

Also, some operators may behave differently depending on how you use them or what values you use together with them. For example:

z = "sample" + "statement"

As you can see, the statement tried to add two strings. In other programming languages, that kind of statement will return an error since their (+) operator is dedicated for addition of numbers only. In Python, it will perform string concatenation that will append the second string to the first. Hence, the value of variable z will become "samplestatement".

On the other hand, you can use the (-) subtraction operator as unary operators. To denote that a variable or number is negative, you can place the subtraction operator before it. For example:

z = 1 - -1

The result will be 2 since 1 minus negative 1 is 2.

The addition operator acts as a unary operator for other languages; however, it behaves differently in Python. In some language, an expression like this: +(-1), will be treated as positive 1. In Python, it will be treated as +1(-1), and if you evaluate that, you will still get negative 1.

To perform a unary positive, you can do this instead:

--1

In that example, Python will read it as −(-1) or -1 * -1 and it will return a positive 1.

Chapter 5: Basic Operators – Part 2

Operators seem to be such a big topic, right? You will be working with them all the time when programming in Python. Once you master or just memorize them all, your overall programming skills will improve since most programming languages have operators that work just like the ones in Python.

And just like a restaurant manager, you would not want to let your chef serve food with only unprocessed ingredients all the time. Not everybody wants salads for their dinner.

Comparison

Aside from performing arithmetic operations and storing values to variables, Python can also allow you to let the computer compare expressions. For example, you can ask your computer if 10 is greater than 20. Since 10 is greater than 20, it will reply with True – meaning the statement you said was correct. If you have compared 20 is greater than 10 instead, it will return a reply that says False.

== : Is Equal

z = x == y

z's value is equal to FALSE.

!= : Is Not Equal

z = x != y

z's value is equal to True.

> : Is Greater Than

z = x > y

z's value is equal to True.

< : Is Less Than

z = x < y

z's value is equal to FALSE.

>= : Is Greater Than or Equal

z = x >= y

z's value is equal to True.

<= : Is Less Than or Equal

z = x <= y

z's value is equal to FALSE.

Note that the last two operators are unlike the combined arithmetic and simple assignment operator.

Logical

Aside from arithmetic and comparison operations, the computer is capable of logical operations, too. Even simple circuitry can do that, but that is another story to tell.

Anyway, do you remember your logic class where your professor talked about truth tables, premises, and propositions? Your computer can understand all of that. Below are the operators you can use to perform logic in Python. In the examples in the list, a is equal to True and b is equal to False.

and : Logical Conjunction AND. It will return only True both the propositions or variable besides it is True. It will return False if any or both the propositions are False.

w = a and a

x = a and b

y = b and a

z = b and b

w is equal to True, x is equal to False, y is equal to False, and z is   equal to False.

or : Logical Disjunction OR. It will return True if any or both of the proposition or variable beside it is True. It will return False if both the propositions are False.

w = a or a

x = a or b

y = b or a

z = b or b

w is equal to True, x is equal to True, y is equal to True, and z is   equal to False.

not : Logical Negation NOT. Any Truth value besides it will be negated. If True is negated, the computer will reply with a False. If False is negated, the computer will reply with a True.

w = not a

x = not b

w is equal to False and x is equal to True.

If you want to perform Logical NAND, you can use Logic Negation NOT and Logical Conjunction AND. For example:

w = not (a and a)

x = not (a and b)

y = not (b and a)

z = not (b and b)

w is equal to False, x is equal to True, y is equal to True, and z is   equal to True.

If you want to perform Logical NOR, you can use Logic Negation NOT and Logical Disjunction OR. For example:

w = not (a or a)

x = not (a or b)

y = not (b or a)

z = not (b or b)

w is equal to False, x is equal to False, y is equal to False, and z is   equal to True.

You can perform other logical operations that do not have Python operators by using conditional statements, which will be discussed later in this book.

Order of Precedence

In case that your statement contains multiple types or instances of operators, Python will evaluate it according to precedence of the operators, which is similar to the PEMDAS rule in Mathematics. It will evaluate the operators with the highest precedence to the lowest. For example:

z = 2 + 10 / 10

Instead of adding 2 and 10 first then dividing the sum by 10, Python will divide 10 by 10 first then add 2 to the quotient instead since division has a higher precedence than subtraction. So, instead of getting 1.2, you will get 3.0. In case that it confuses you, imagine that Python secretly adds parentheses to the expression. The sample above is the same as:

z = 2 + (10 / 10)

If two operators with the same level of precedence exist in one statement, Python will evaluate the first operator that appears from the left. For example:

z = 10 / 10 * 2

The value of variable z will be 2.

Take note that any expressions inside parentheses or nested deeper in parentheses will have higher precedence than those expressions outside the parentheses. For example:

z = 2 / ((1 + 1) * (2 – 4))

Even though the division operator came first and has higher precedence than addition and subtraction, Python evaluated the ones inside the parentheses first and evaluated the division operation last. So, it added 1 and 1, subtracted 4 from 2, multiplied the sum and difference of the two previous operations, and then divided the product from 2. The value of variable z became -0.5.

Below is a reference for the precedence of the operations. The list is sorted from operations with high precedence to operators with low precedence.

> **Exponents**
> **Unary**
> **Multiplication, Division, Modulo, and Floor Division**
> **Addition, and Subtraction**
> **Bitwise**
> **Comparison**
> **Assignment**
> **Identity**
> **Membership**
> **Logical**

Truth Values

The values True and False are called truth values – or sometimes called Boolean data values. The value True is equal to 1 and the value False is equal to 0. That means that you can treat or use 1 as the truth value True and 0 as the truth value False. Try comparing those two values in your interpreter. Code the following:

True == 1

False == 0

The interpreter will return a value of True – meaning, you can interchange them in case a situation arises. However, it is advisable that that you use them like that sparingly.

Another thing you should remember is that the value True and False are case sensitive. True != TRUE or False != false. Aside from that, True and False are Python keywords. You cannot create variables named after them.

You might be wondering about the use of truth values in programming. The answer is, you can use them to control your programs using conditional or flow control tools. With them, you can make your program execute statements when a certain condition arises. And that will be discussed on the next chapter.

Chapter 6: Functions, Flow Control, and User Input

With statements, you have learned to tell instructions to the computer using Pythons. As of now, all you know is how to assign variables and manipulate expressions. And the only command you know is print. Do you think you can make a decent program with those alone? Maybe, but you do not need to rack your brains thinking of one.

In this chapter, you will learn about functions and flow control. This time, you will need to leave the interpreter or Interactive mode. Open your source code editor since you will be programming blocks of codes during this section.

Functions

Statements are like sentences in a book or steps in a recipe. On the other hand, functions are like paragraphs or a recipe in a recipe book. Functions are blocks of code with multiple statements that will perform a specific goal or goals when executed. Below is an example:

def recipe1():

>**print("Fried Fish Recipe")**
>
>**print("Ingredients:")**
>
>**print("Fish")**
>
>**print("Salt")**
>
>**print("Steps:")**
>
>**print("1. Rub salt on fish.")**
>
>**print("2. Fry fish.")**
>
>**print("3. Serve.")**

The function's purpose is to print the recipe for Fried Fish. To create a function, you will need to type the keyword def (for define) then the name of the function. In the example, the name of the function is recipe1. The parentheses are important to be present there. It has its purpose, but for now, leave it alone.

After the parentheses, a colon was placed. The colon signifies that a code block will be under the function.

To include statements inside that code block, you must indent it. In the example, one indentation or tab was used. To prevent encountering errors, make sure that all the statements are aligned and have the same number of indentations.

To end the code block for the function, all you need is to type a statement that has the same indentation level of the function declaration.

By the way, all the statements inside a function code block will not be executed until the function is called or invoked. To invoke the function, all you need is to call it using its name. To invoke the function recipe1, type this:

recipe1()

And that is how simple functions work.

Flow Control

It is sad that only one recipe can be displayed by the sample function. It would be great if your program can display more recipes. And letting the user choose the recipe that they want to be displayed on the program would be cool. But how can you do that?

You can do that by using flow control tools in Python. With them, you can direct your program to do something if certain conditions are met. In the case of the recipe listing program, you can apply flow control and let them see the recipes by requesting it.

If Statement

The simplest control flow tool you can use for this type of project is the if statement. Have you been wondering about truth values? Now, you can use them with if statements.

An *if statement* is like a program roadblock. If the current condition of your program satisfies its requirements, then it will let it access the block of statements within it. It is like a function with no names, and instead of being invoked to work, it needs you to satisfy the conditions set to it. For example:

a = 2

if a == 2:

> **print("You satisfied the condition!")**

> **print("This is another statement that will be executed!")**

if a == (1 + 1):

> **print("You satisfied the condition again!")**

> **print("I will display the recipe for Fried Fish!")**

> **recipe1()**

If you will translate the first if statement in English, it will mean that: if variable a is equals to 2, then print the sentence inside the parentheses. Another way to translate it is: if the comparison between variable a and the number 2 returns True, then print the sentence inside the parentheses.

As you can see, the colon is there and the statements below the if statement are indented, too. It really is like a function.

User Input

You can now control the flow of your program and create functions. Now, about the recipe program, how can the user choose the recipe he wants to view? That can be done by using the input() command. You can use it like this:

a = input("Type your choice here and press enter: ")

Once Python executes that line, it will stop executing statements. And provide a prompt that says "Type your choice here: ". During that moment, the user will be given a chance to type something in the program. If the user press enter, Python will store and assign the characters the user typed on the program to variable a. Once that process is done, Python will resume executing the statements after the input statement.

In some cases, programmers use the input command to pause the program and wait for the user to press enter. You can do that by just placing input() on a line.

With that, you can make a program that can capture user input and can change its flow whenever it gets the right values from the user. You can create a recipe program that allows users to choose the recipe they want. Here is the code. Analyze it. And use the things you have learned to improve it. Good luck.

print("Enter the number of the recipe you want to read.")

print("1 - Fried Fish")

print("2 - Fried Egg")

print("Enter any character to Exit")

choice = input("Type a Number and Press Enter: ")

if choice == "1":

    print("Fried Fish Recipe")

    print("Ingredients:")

    print("Fish")

```python
        print("Salt")

        print("Steps:")

        print("1. Rub salt on fish.")

        print("2. Fry fish.")

        print("3. Serve.")

        pause = input("Press enter when you are done reading.")


if choice == "2":

        print("Fried Egg Recipe")

        print("Ingredients:")

        print("Egg")

        print("Salt")

        print("Steps:")

        print("1. Fry egg.")

        print("2. Sprinkle Salt.")

        print("3. Serve.")

        pause = input("Press enter when you are done reading.")
```

Conclusion

Thank you again for purchasing this book!

I hope this book was able to help you to learn the basics of Python programming.

The next step is to learn more about Python! You should have expected that coming.

Kidding aside, with the current knowledge you have in Python programming, you can make any programs like that with ease. But of course, there are still lots of things you need to learn about the language such as loops, classes, and etcetera.

Finally, if you enjoyed this book, please take the time to share your thoughts and post a review on Amazon. We do our best to reach out to readers and provide the best value we can. Your positive review will help us achieve that. It'd be greatly appreciated!

Thank you and good luck!

Book 2
HTML Professional
Programming Made Easy

By Sam Key

Expert HTML Programming Language Success in a Day for any Computer Users

Table Of Contents

Introduction

I want to thank you and congratulate you for purchasing the book, *Professional HTML Programming Made Easy: Expert HTML Programming Language Success In A Day for any Computer User!*

This book contains proven steps and strategies on how to create a web page in just a day. And if you have a lot of time in a day, you will be able to create a decent and informative website in two or three days.

HTML programming or development lessons are sometimes used as an introductory resource to programming and is a prerequisite to learning web development. In this book, you will be taught of the fundamentals of HTML. Mastering the contents of this book will make web development easier for you and will allow you to grasp some of the basics of computer programming.

To get ready for this book, you will need a desktop or laptop. That is all. You do not need to buy any expensive HTML or website development programs. And you do not need to rent a server or subscribe to a web hosting service. If you have questions about those statements, the answers are in the book.

Thanks again for purchasing this book. I hope you enjoy it!

Chapter 1: Getting Started with HTML

This book will assume that you have no prior knowledge on HTML. Do not skip reading any chapters or this book if you plan to learn about CSS, JavaScript, or any other languages that is related to web development.

HTML is a markup language. HTML defines what will be displayed on your browser and how it will be displayed. To program or code HTML, all you need is a text editor. If your computer is running on a Windows operating system, you can use Notepad to create or edit HTML files. Alternatively, if your computer is a Mac, you can use TextEdit instead.

Why is this book telling you to use basic text editors? Why are expert web developers using HTML creation programs such as Adobe Dreamweaver to create their pages? Those programs are supposed to make HTML coding easier, right?

You do not need them yet. Using one will only confuse you, especially if you do not know the fundamentals of HTML. Aside from that, web designing programs such as Adobe Dreamweaver are not all about dragging and dropping items on a web page. You will also need to be capable of manually writing the HTML code that you want on your page. That is why those programs have different views like Design and Code views. And most of them time, advanced developers stay and work more using the Code view, which is similar to a typical text editing program.

During your time learning HTML using this book, create a folder named HTML on your desktop. As you progress, you will see snippets of HTML code written here. You can try them out using your text editor and browser. You can save them as HTML files, place them into the HTML folder, and open them on your browser to see what those snippets of codes will do.

Your First HTML Page

Open your text editor and type the following in it:

Hello World!
After writing that line on your text editor, save it. On the save file dialog box, change the name of the file as firstexample.html. Do not forget the .html part. That part will serve as your file's file extension. It denotes that the file that you have saved is an HTML file and can be opened by the web browsers you have in

your computer. Make sure that your program was able to save it as an .html file. Some text editor programs might still automatically add another file extension on your file name, so if that happens, you will not be open that file in your browser normally.

By the way, you do not need to upload your HTML file on a website or on the internet to view it. As long as your computer can access it, you can open it. And since your first HTML page will be in your computer, you can open it with your browser. After all, a web site can be viewed as a folder on the internet that contains HTML files that you can open.

When saving the file, make sure that it is being saved as plain text and not rich or formatted text. By default, programs such as Microsoft Word or WordPad save text files as formatted. If you saved the file as formatted, your browser might display the HTML code you have written incorrectly.

To open that file, you can try one of the three common ways. The first method is to double click or open the file normally. If you were able to save the file with the correct file extension, your computer will automatically open a browser to access the file.

The second method is to use the context menu (if you are using Windows). Right click on the file, and hover on the open with option. The menu will expand, and the list of programs that can open an HTML file will be displayed to you. Click on the browser that you want to use to open the file.

The third method is to open your browser. After that, type the local file address of your file. If you are using Windows 7 and you saved the file on the HTML folder in your desktop, then you can just type in C:\Users\User\Desktop\HTML\firstexample.html. The folder User may change depending on the account name you are using on your computer to login.

Once you have opened the file, it will show you the text you have written on it. Congratulations, you have already created a web page. You can just type paragraphs of text in the file, and it will be displayed by your browsers without problem. It is not the fanciest method, but it is the start of your journey to learn HTML.

You might be wondering, is it that easy? To be honest, yes. Were you expecting complex codes? Well, that will be tackled on the next chapter. And just to give you a heads up, it will not be complex.

This chapter has just given you an idea what is an HTML file and how you create, edit, and open one in your computer. The next chapter will discuss about tags, attributes, and elements.

Chapter 2: Elements, Properties, Tags, and Attributes

Of course, you might be already thinking: "Web pages do not contain text only, right?" Yes, you are right. In this part of the book, you will have a basic idea about how HTML code works, and how you can place some links on your page.

A web page is composed of elements. A picture on a website's gallery is an element. A paragraph on a website's article is also an element. A hyperlink that directs to another page is an element, too. But how can you do that with text alone? If you can create a web page by just using a text editor, how can you insert images on it?

Using Tags

Well, you can do that by using tags and attributes. By placing tags on the start and end of a text, you will be able to indicate what element it is. It might sound confusing, so below is an example for you to visualize and understand it better and faster:

<p>This is a paragraph that is enclosed on a paragraph tag. This is another sentence. And another sentence.</p>

In the example, the paragraph is enclosed with <p> and </p>. Those two are called HTML tags. If you enclose a block of text inside those two, the browser will understand that the block of text is a paragraph element.

Before you go in further about other HTML tags, take note that there is syntax to follow when enclosing text inside HTML tags. First, an HTML tag has two parts. The first part is the opening or starting tag. And the second part is the closing or ending tag.

The opening tag is enclosed on angled brackets or chevrons (the ones that you use to denote inequality – less and greater than signs). The closing tag, on the other hand, is also enclosed on angled brackets, but it includes a forward slash before the tag itself. The forward slash denotes that the tag is an ending tag.

Those two tags must come in pairs when you use them. However, there are HTML tags that do not require them. And they are called null or void tags. This will be discussed in another lesson. For now, stick on learning the usual HTML tags which require both opening and closing tags.

Attributes

When it comes to inserting images and links in your HTML file, you will need to use attributes. Elements have properties. The properties of each element may vary. For example, paragraph elements do not have the HREF property that anchor elements have (the HREF property and anchor element will be discussed shortly).

To change or edit those properties, you need to assign values using attributes tags. Remember, to indicate an element, use tags; to change values of the properties of elements, use attributes. However, the meanings and relations of those terms might change once you get past HTML and start learning doing CSS and JavaScript. Nevertheless, hold on to that basic idea first until you get further in web development.

Anyway, you will not actually use attributes, but you will need to indicate or assign values on them. Below is an example on how to insert a link on your web page that you will require you to assign a value on an attribute:

<a href="www.google.com" >Google</a>
If ever you copied that, pasted or written it on your HTML file, and open your file on a browser, you will see this:

Google

In the example above, the anchor or <a> HTML tag is used. Use the anchor tag when you want to embed a hyperlink or link in your page. Any text between the opening and closing tags of the anchor tag will become the text that will appear as the hyperlink. In the example, it is the word Google that is place between the tags and has appeared on the browser as the link.

You might have noticed the href="www.google.com" part. That part of the line determines on what page your link will direct to when you click it. That part is an example of attribute value assignment. HREF or hypertext reference is an attribute of the anchor tag.

By default, the anchor tag's value is "" or blank. In case that you do not assign any value to that attribute when you use the anchor tag, the anchor element will not become a hyperlink. Try copying and saving this line on your HTML file.

```
<a>Google</a>
```

When you open or refresh your HTML file, it will only show the word Google. It will not be underlined or will have a font color of blue. It will be just a regular text. If you hover on it, your mouse pointer will not change into the hand icon; if you click it, your browser will not do anything because the HREF value is blank.

By the way, when you assign a value on an element's or tag's attribute, you must follow proper syntax. The attribute value assignment must be inside the opening tag's chevrons and must be after the text inside the tag.

The attribute assignment must be separated from the tag with a space or spaces. The attribute's name must be type first. It must be followed by an equals sign. Then the value you want to assign to the attribute must follow the equals sign, and must be enclosed with double quotes or single quotes.

Take note, even if the number of spaces between the opening tag and the attribute assignment does not matter much, it is best that you only use one spaces for the sake of readability.

Also, you can place a space between the attribute name and the equals sign or a space between the equals sign and the value that you want to assign to the attribute. However, it is best to adhere to standard practice by not placing a space between them.

When it comes to the value that you want to assign, you can either enclosed them in double or single quotes, but you should never enclose them on a single quote and a double quote or vice versa. If you start with a single quote, end with a single quote, too. Using different quotes will bring problems to your code that will affect the way your browser will display your HTML file.

Nesting HTML Tags

What if you want to insert a link inside your paragraph? How can you do that? Well, in HTML, you can place or nest tags inside tags. Below is an example:

```
<p>This is a paragraph. If you want to go to Google, click this <a
href="www.google.com" >link</a>.</p>
```

If you save that on your HTML file and open your file in your browser, it will appear like this:

This is a paragraph. If you want to go to Google, click this <u>link</u>.

When coding HTML, you will be nesting a lot of elements. Always remember that when nesting tags, never forget the location of the start and closing tags. Make sure that you always close the tags you insert inside a tag before closing the tag you are placing a tag inside on. If you get them mixed up, problems in your page's display will occur. Those tips might sound confusing, so below is an example of a mixed up tag:

<p>This is a paragraph. If you want to go to Google, click this <a href="www.google.com" >link</p>. And this is an example of tags getting mixed up and closed improperly.</a>

In the example, the closing tag for the paragraph tag came first before the closing tag of the anchor tag. If you copied, saved, and opened that, this is what you will get:

This is a paragraph. If you want to go to Google, click this <u>link</u>

<u>. And this is an example of tag that was mixed up and closed improperly.</u>

Since paragraphs are block elements (elements that will be always displayed on the next line and any element after them will be displayed on the next line), the last sentence was shifted to the next line. That is because the code has terminated the paragraph tag immediately.

Also, the anchor tag was closed on the end of the paragraph. Because of that, the word link up to the last word of the last sentence became a hyperlink. You should prevent that kind of mistakes, especially if you are going to code a huge HTML file and are using other complex tags that require a lot of nesting such as table tags. In addition, always be wary of the number of starting and ending tags you use. Missing tags or excess tags can also ruin your web page and fixing and looking for them is a pain.

This chapter has taught you the basic ideas about elements, properties, tags, and attributes. In coding HTML, you will be mostly fiddling around with them. In the next chapter, you will learn how to code a proper HTML document.

Chapter 3: The Standard Structure of HTML

As of now, all you can do are single lines on your HTML file. Though, you might have already tried making a page full of paragraphs and links – thanks to your new found knowledge about HTML tags and attributes. And you might be already hungry to learn more tags that you can use and attributes that you can assign values with.

However, before you tackle those tags and attributes, you should learn about the basic structure of an HTML document. The HTML file you have created is not following the standards of HTML. Even though it does work on your browser, it is not proper to just place random HTML tags on your web page on random places.

In this chapter, you will learn about the html, head, and body tags. And below is the standard structure of an HTML page where those three tags are used:

```
<!DOCTYPE html>
<html>
<head></head>
<body></body>
</html>
```

The Body and the Head

You can split an HTML document in two. The first part is composed of the things that the browser displays on your screen. And the second part is composed of the things that you will not see but is important to your document.

Call the first part as your HTML page's body. And call the second part as your HTML page's head. Every web page that you can see on the net are composed of these two parts. The tags that you have learned in the previous chapter are part of your HTML's body.

As you can see on the example, the head and body tag are nested inside the html tag. The head goes in first, while the body is the last one to appear. The order of the two is essential to your web page.

When coding in HTML, you should always place or nest all the tags or elements that your visitors will see on your HTML's body tag. On the other hand, any script or JavaScript code and styling line or CSS line that your visitors will not see must go into the head tag.

Scripts and styling lines must be read first by your browser. Even before the browser displays all the elements in your body tag, it must be already stylized and the scripts should be ready. And that is why the head tag goes first before the body.

If you place the styling lines on the end of the page, the browser may behave differently. For example, if the styling lines are placed at the end, the browser will display the elements on the screen first, and then once it reads the styling lines, the appearance of the page will change. On the other hand, if a button on your page gets clicked before the scripts for it was loaded because the scripts are placed on the end of the document, the browser will return an error.

Browsers and Checking the Source Code

Fortunately, if you forget to place the html, head, and body tags, modern browsers will automatically generate them for you. For example, try opening the HTML file that you created without the three tags with Google Chrome.

Once you open your file, press the F12 key to activate the developer console. As you can see, the html, head, and body tags were already generated for you in order to display your HTML file properly.

By the way, checking source codes is an important method that you should always use if you want to learn or imitate a website's HTML code. You can easily do it by using the developer console on Chrome or by using the context menu on other browsers and clicking on the View Page Source or View Source option.

Document Type Declaration

HTML has undergone multiple versions. As of now, the latest version is HTML5. With each version, some tags are introduced while some are deprecated. And some versions come with specifications that make them behave differently from each other. Because of that, HTML documents must include a document type declaration to make sure that your markup will be displayed just the way you wanted them to appear on your visitors' screens.

However, you do not need to worry about this a lot since it will certainly stick with HTML5, which will not be discussed in full in this book. In HTML5, document type declaration is useless, but is required. To satisfy this, all you need to do is place this on the beginning of your HTML files:

```
<!DOCTYPE html>
```

With all of those laid out, you can now create proper HTML documents. In the following chapters, the book will focus on providing you the tags that you will use the most while web developing.

Chapter 4: More HTML Tags

Now, it is time to make your HTML file to appear like a typical web page on the internet. And you can do that by learning the tags and attributes that are used in websites you stumble upon while you surf the web.

The Title Tag

First of all, you should give your web page a title. You can do that by using the <title> tag. The title of the page can be seen on the title bar and tab on your browser. If you bookmark your page, it will become the name of the bookmark. Also, it will appear on your taskbar if the page is active.

When using the title tag, place it inside the head tag. Below is an example:

```
<head>
        <title>This Is My New Web Page</title>
</head>
```

The Header Tags

If you want to organize the hierarchy of your titles and text on your web page's article, then you can take advantage of the header tags. If you place a line of text inside header tags, its formatting will change. Its font size will become bigger and its font weight (thickness) will become heavier. For example:

```
<h1> This Is the Title of This Article</h1>
<p>This is the introductory paragraph. This is another sentence. And this is the last sentence.</p>
```

If you try this example, this is what you will get:

This Is the Title of This Article

This is the introductory paragraph. This is another sentence. And this is the last sentence.

There are six levels of heading tags and they are: <h1>,<h2>,<h3>,<h4>,<h5>, and <h6>. Each level has different formatting. And as the level gets higher, the lesser formatting will be applied.

The Image Tag

First, start with pictures. You can insert pictures in your web page by using the <img> tag. By the way, the <img> tag is one of HTML tags that do not need closing tags, which are called null or empty tags. And for you to see how it works, check the example below:

<img
src="http://upload.wikimedia.org/wikipedia/commons/thumb/8/80/Wikipedia
-logo-v2.svg/150px-Wikipedia-logo-v2.svg.png" >

If you try that code and opened your HTML file, the Wikipedia logo will appear. As you can see, the <img> tag did not need a closing tag to work. As long as you place a valid value on its src (source) attribute, then an image will appear on your page. In case an image file is not present on the URL you placed on the source attribute, then a broken image picture will appear instead.

Image Format Tips

By the way, the <img> tag can display pictures with the following file types: PNG, JPEG or JPG, and GIF. Each image type has characteristics that you can take advantage of. If you are going to post photographs, it is best to convert them to JPG file format. The JPG offers decent file compression that can reduce the size of your photographs without losing too much quality.

If you need lossless quality or if you want to display a photo or image as is, then you should use PNG. The biggest drawback on PNG is that old browsers cannot read PNG images. But that is almost a thing of a past since only handful people use old versions of browsers.

On the other hand, if you want animated images on your site, then use GIFs. However, take note that the quality of GIF is not that high. The number of colors it can display is few unlike PNG and JPG. But because of that, its size is comparatively smaller than the two formats, which is why some web developers convert their sites' logos as GIF to conserve space and reduce loading time.

The Ordered and Unordered List

Surely, you will place lists on your web pages sooner or later. In HTML, you can create two types of lists: ordered and unordered. Ordered lists generate

41

alphanumeric characters to denote sequence on your list while unordered lists generate symbols that only change depending on the list level.

To create ordered lists, use the <ol> and <li> tag. The <ol> tag defines that the list will be an ordered one, and the <li> or list item tag defines that its content is considered a list item on the list. Below is an example:

```
<h1>Animals</h1>
<ol>
        <li>dog</li>
        <li>cat</li>
        <li>mouse</li>
</ol>
```
This will be the result of that example:

Animals

1. dog

2. cat

3. mouse

On the other hand, if you want an unordered list, you will need to use the <ul> tag. Like the <ol> tag, you will still need to use the <li> tag to denote the list items. Below is an example:

```
<h1>Verbs</h1>
<ul>
        <li>walk</li>
        <li>jog</li>
        <li>run</li>
</ul>
```
This will be the result of that example:

Verbs

• walk

• jog

- run

Instead of numbers, the list used bullets instead. If ever you use the <li> tag without <ol> or <ul>, browsers will usually create them as unordered lists.

Nesting Lists

You can nest lists in HTML to display child lists. If you do that, the browser will accommodate it and apply the necessary tabs for the child list items. If you nest unordered lists, the bullets will be changed to fit the child list items. Below is an example:

```
<h1>Daily Schedule</h1>
<ul>
      <li>Morning</li>

      <ul>
            <li>Jog</li>
            <li>Shower</li>
            <li>Breakfast</li>
      </ul>
      <li>Afternoon</li>
      <ul>
            <li>Lunch</li>
            <li>Watch TV</li>
      </ul>
      <li>Evening</li>
      <ul>
            <li>Dinner</li>
            <li>Sleep</li>
      </ul>
</ul>
```

This will be the result of that example:

Daily Schedule

- Morning

  o Jog

- Shower

- Breakfast

• Afternoon

- Lunch

- Watch TV

• Evening

- Dinner

- Sleep

And with that, you should be ready to create a decent website of your own. But for now, practice using those tags. And experiment with them.

Conclusion

Thank you again for purchasing this book!

I hope this book was able to help you to become knowledgeable when it comes to HTML development. With the fundamentals you have learned, you can easily explore the vast and enjoyable world of web development. And that is no exaggeration.

The next step is to learn more tags and check out websites' sources. Also, look for HTML development tips. Then learn more about HTML5 and schema markup. Those things will help you create richer web sites that are semantically optimized.

On the other hand, if you want to make your website to look cool, then you can jump straight to leaning CSS or Cascading Style Sheets. Cascading Style Sheets will allow you to define the appearance of all or each element in your web page. You can change font size, weight, color, and family of all the text on your page in a whim. You can even create simple animations that can make your website look modern and fancy.

If you want your website to be interactive, then you can start learning client side scripting with JavaScript or Jscript too. Scripts will provide your web pages with functions that can make it more alive. An example of a script function is when you press a button on your page, a small window will popup.

Once you master all of that, then it will be the best time for you to start learning server side scripting such as PHP or ASP. With server side scripting, you can almost perform everything on websites. You can take information from forms and save them to your database. Heck, you can even create dynamic web pages. Or even add chat functions on your website.

Finally, if you enjoyed this book, please take the time to share your thoughts and post a review on Amazon. We do our best to reach out to readers and provide the best value we can. Your positive review will help us achieve that. It'd be greatly appreciated!

Thank you and good luck!

Check Out My Other Books

Below you'll find some of my other popular books that are popular on Amazon and Kindle as well. Simply click on the links below to check them out. Alternatively, you can visit my author page on Amazon to see other work done by me.

C Programming Success in a Day

Android Programming in a Day

C Programming Professional Made Easy

C ++ Programming Success in a Day

Python Programming in a Day

PHP Programming Professional Made Easy

JavaScript Programming Made Easy

CSS Programming Professional Made Easy

Windows 8 Tips for Beginners

If the links do not work, for whatever reason, you can simply search for these titles on the Amazon website to find them.

www.ingramcontent.com/pod-product-compliance
Lightning Source LLC
Chambersburg PA
CBHW060929050326
40689CB00013B/3026